Something Completely Different!

Poems, Proverbs, Rhymes

by Chris Dyer

Monday Creek Publishing
Ohio USA

Printed in the United States of America

Monday Creek Publishing, Ohio, USA
mondaycreekpublishing.com

ISBN-13: 978-0692878279
ISBN-10: 0692878270

Something Completely Different!

Dedication

I would like to dedicate this book to the Phoenix. A beautiful, mythical bird, with plumage unparalleled by any other creature, a beauty so great, that it must turn to ashes and regenerate. It is sadly a mythical creature that only exists in our dreams and imagination, or is it? Imagination fuels our thoughts and even imagination and thoughts must have an origin! When the Phoenix turns to ashes we must not shed a tear, but live in hope that the rebirth is complete and will bring us even greater joy. The Phoenix lives and has fired my imagination and the ashes burned my soul. Cameras flash and videos play, but they only see the brilliant feathers, not the blessedness before them. It is said that the tear of the Phoenix has magical powers, but still you only see the plumage.

Five leaves left

One leaf falls,

I watch,

I stand beneath her,

Her inhibitions gone,

No longer dressed in green,

Coy and vibrant,

Another falls,

I watch,

Her slender form near naked,

I watch,

Graceful, beautiful,

I watch,

Standing still her five leaves left.

Evolution?

Lie there and see,

Listen to the wind,

It tells its story.

Its journey from afar,

Water never still rushes by,

Fires bring health yet destroys,

Earth brings forth life,

Man brings devastation.

Gus

I know a dog his name is Gus,

He isn't big but quite robust,

He's sort of brown but has some white,

He's very good and never fights,

His favourite thing must be his ball,

And chasing up and down the hall,

From him a child can take a bone,

And Gus will never even moan,

He loves the postman he loves them all,

But most of all he loves his ball.

The office party

Stagger drunken fool,

Your fix has been too great,

Fall upon the pavement swimming in your own vomit,

Watch the faces as they pass,

Disgust upon their face,

Drag yourself to your home where your wife awaits,

Her eyes full of fear and loathing,

Too drunk to hide the indiscretion,

Slap her with your own guilt,

Watch as the blood runs from her nose,

Hear the door slam behind her,

The taxi waiting concern upon the drivers face,

Now sitting alone eating your take away,

Happy New Year.

The gin bottle

I sit,

One hand left and one hand right,

The top is now screwed down quite tight.

Pissed again.

The plight of Ethel

Ethel is a spider,

She's living in our loo,

We've got to knock the toilet down,

Oh what will Ethel do?

Ethel's packed her suitcase,

She's looking very sad.

She has to find another home,

Oh really that's too bad.

Nyoka

The cobra sat upon the hedge and looked at me,
No fear from either side,
The natives screamed *bwana apana nyoka,*
nyoka, mbaya sana.
No snake, snake very bad!
Very bad? Why it is just another creature,
I reach forward with my phone set to camera,
It looks at me, but I move slowly
so as not to threaten,
It lifts its head just a few inches,
wary but still not aggressive,
I take the picture and it relaxes
as I simply gaze at it,
I do not like but do not dislike snakes,
I can however see their beauty,
The subtle change of hue as
the sun catches its scales,
The way it moves drawing S's in its wake.
It retreats and disappears beneath the hedge,
Camouflaged from prying eyes,

I search each day to see it but it does not return,

Then as I walk the fields one day I look down

and there it is,

Involuntarily I start but it only looks

at me this time,

I am intrigued, I walk it follows,

I stop and so does it,

I walk towards it. It moves away keeping the few

feet between us,

For I realise it is only a few feet

no more than four,

It is as curious of me now as I was of it then,

I walk the field and it follows,

Always keeping that few feet away

but always there,

Suddenly it takes off at incredible speed,

I realise that I could not have out run it,

It disappears into the hedge and was gone,

I wonder if it managed the picture it wanted.

One

One heart held,
One soul offered,
One love forgiven,
One love took all.

Lone wolf

Why this ache so sharp so gay,

And yet alone so cold so grey,

The holding back, to test restraint,

My walls of black so bright you paint

The lone wolf in his cloak of worldly sneers,

Pacing slowly through the years,

Pray don't look on him with such disdain,

For in his eyes are tears of pain.

For though through wooded hills he slinks,

Inside his heart like lamb he thinks.

Reach out slowly an empty space,
The pillow that once held her face,

Now lies pristine as white as snow,
Just one moment just one thought,

Turn no warmth that you once held,
No tingle as soft hair brushes skin,

No elation as you listen to her soft breath,
Even gone the irritation as the cover
dragged from you,

No sweet kiss as you awake,
No smile as her arm reaches over
you to pull you tight,

Just another endless night.

Remember

No words to write from empty heart,

No soul when souls are torn apart,

To feel the void of pure despair,

To look not touch a fuse so fair,

Remember words remember me,

In years I may then be set free.

Life is like a bowl of cherries.... The problem is someone has eaten mine and left me the stones!

The truth is like standing in a dark room... Someone always comes along and switches the light on.

Friendship is like being on a sandy beach when you reach for it, it can so easily slip through your fingers.

You can be in a room full of people but as lonely as hell.

The sun may shine on the righteous but they burn just the same as you and I.

Friendship is like a fur coat you should put it on when it's cold and give it when someone's freezing.

When I first met you I thought you were so good... I'm glad you turned out not to be its so much more fun.

Love is great it's like sitting with a warm cat on your lap...until it gets its claws out.

Manners may make man...but money makes you attractive.

Your body oozes sensuality...by the way your deodorants not working.

If eyes were diamonds... you'd be the crown jewels.

The hit

The hit man stares through cold blue eyes,
He watches 'neath the cloudless skies,
Stealing silently through the night,
Beneath his coat a gun held tight,
Jewels of sweat upon his faceless brow,
The trigger squeezed, the pain comes now,
Yours now over.
His has just begun.

Stable

Cut the strings, shake nature,

Smell the scents of days gone by,

Of spring of warmth,

The feel of summer in cold hands,

The soft whicker that calls,

The icy breath as you laugh,

Soothing as you brush sleek hair,

Nuzzled by a velvet nose.

Lost for words

What are words, redundant now,

Replaced by the keys and a screen,

No touch to emphasise a point,

No smile where one can sense,

A future of screens and fast fingers,

Perhaps we shall change all,

Abbreviate everything for speed,

Today I spoke to someone,

I did not know them but they grabbed my words,

Old and lonely, behind the times? Perhaps?

Or maybe they realise that to move ahead we

must step back,

Just a few words and I saw their youth return,

When you walk think,

The person you have passed by as you tap away,

Clutching fiercely to your little rectangle,

Just a word or two to make a day,

And all for free.

Wonder

I saw one flake of snow as it drifted to the ground,

How far had it come?

Yet it made no sound,

As soft as velvet, cold as ice,

I looked towards the sky to see,

Another snowflake drift to me.

Save me

I am quite grey with a little pink,

I really love to have a drink,

The ground that trembles as I stride,

I have much thought, I walk with pride,

You look at me but do not see,

That once described my majesty,

A refrain I have to say,

Will I survive another day,

Not only me, for there are lots,

From which you make or put in pots,

You pray your worth for soon you'll find,

No more of me and my own kind.

Then tell your children it was you,

That would not stand and help renew,

But think of this a clever man,

When I speak won't understand,

Yet I know every word you say,

What will you tell when comes the day.

The gift

One precious gift given yet not owned
One to be cherished unselfishly
One minute missed a tragedy
One tear shed in joy is one tear worthwhile,
One thousand shed in sorrow and all are wasted,
One heart that fills with love beats life,
One heart that fills with sorrow lies still,
One hand that reaches out succeeds,
One hand that stays does little,
One life is all we have,
One life too soon,
One love is given,
One love to fall,
One love forgiven,
One love took all.

See me

What could I be?

One moment there,

Then none can see,

And yet I do not hide from thee,

I cover all,

A wall so thick,

That you can hide, a magic trick?

On land as well, as ocean swell,

On hill and dale on mountains hold,

Sometimes wet and sometimes cold.

What could I be?

Such joy comes from the feel of

grass beneath the feet,

The warmth of the sun,

A star that shines endlessly,

The full moon bright,

I pray we leave it for those who come.

I sit beside another man,

He has two arms and legs,

His heart beats as does mine,

His blood is red,

He dies as do I,

He breathes as do I,

We both think,

Our lives are different,

Our culture un-similar,

But we are still men.

Together.

Bring forth thy passion,

Comforting in your warmth,

Restful in your arms,

Supporting as you fall.

And blissful in your company.

Wondering

What is love?

Beauty?

Money?

Truth?

Lies?

Perhaps comfort?

The net

We never meet we never see,

And yet you are a friend to me,

Not once your voice has made a sound,

Or together walked around,

No chat with coffee have we had,

The world I think is going mad.

The internet.

Surgery

The surgeon's knife cuts deep.
Into the flesh, through skin and muscle,

Straight and true it will leave little scar,
Stitched and dressed, soon forgotten,

The lovers knife cuts deeper still,
Into the soul through to the heart,

No stitches here, no dressing applied,
No scar seen but always felt.

Final bliss

When all is still when all is calm
When day meets night when night meets day

When life is hard when life is gay
When I see you when you see me

When all is light when all is grey
When I hear when I say

When comes the end when comes the start
When time to join when time to part

For soon together all shall be
When reached the final ecstasy.

The dream

I look upon your smile,
I sense your breath upon my neck,

Your hair soft against my shoulder
cascading upon my chest,

I wonder at your eyes,
I tremble as your sleeping hand rests upon mine,

The warm touch of your skin,
smooth and irresistible.

My fingers trace the curve of your hips,
My heart beats faster as I gaze upon your
slender legs,

Your lips a promise as yet unfulfilled,
I turn and wake afraid to turn back,
A dream?

Question ??

What are we but an empty vessel?
Concerned egos,

Looking at each shop window
to glimpse a reflection,

What are we when giving our words of passion
Lies to meet our own ends,

What are we?

From far

Once from far I heard a voice,
Sweet, clever, captivating,
Such longing, such loneliness,
Beautiful, creative, caring,
Once from far I heard a voice.
Soft, caressing, smiling
Such thoughts to move the soul.
Sexual, mesmerising, exciting,
Once from afar I heard a voice,
Beautiful, loving, hypnotising.
Challenging, intellectual, hypocritical,
Once from afar I heard a voice.

When all is lost, when all is gone,

Do I sing or cry my song?

Do I laugh and turn away?

Return as if it was yesterday?

Can I smile or can I weep?

Yet so tired but cannot sleep.

All around

I am thrown, I am cut, I am shaped,

I am a weapon, I am heat,

I am played with,

I am sat upon,

I am admired,

I am air,

I am indispensable,

I am small,

I am huge,

I am all around,

What am I?

Seven

Seven would be three,

If it was not seven,

A heart would be a pump,

If it was not a heart,

Love would be dark,

If it was not light.

Beauty

Beauty comes in many forms,

Words can be enchanting,

A mountain range stunning,

A woman breathtaking,

And yet the one thing given to us,

The one thing with such potential to be beautiful,

Is abused...

the human mind.

The still of night, the silence,
Thoughts that come and drift away into the darkness,

No vision, no light to see,
From nothingness a glimpse of me,

Confusing images rush before my eyes,
Emotions churning,

Nothing defined, nothing solved,
I crave the light as relief,

The sun will bring a new dawn.

A wise man thinks a fool shouts,

A proud man struts a humble man walks,

A greedy man gathers a generous man offers,

A kind man lifts an uncaring man passes by,

We have yet to realise that we all head in the

same direction.

Clouds scud across the sky,

Another day is passing by,

It was not me that made the clock,

As time upon my door does knock,

Why are we so concerned with age,

It is the turning of a page,

Our knowledge grows as does our hope,

Another day with which to cope.

Do you forget you work for me?
Without my vote you would not be,
Yet now as children starve and cry,
You bring more war I wonder why.

Time

What is time? A passing click,

A clock we watch, a man made trick,

Time may go but never comes,

The hands still move the heart still drums,

Beauty found and beauty lost,

Time passes by and at such cost,

Became complete but no one cared,

Never would I bend my knee,

Admit defeat to them or me,

My strength it comes from deep inside,

I shall still as myself preside,

So what of now to sink or drown?

I'll show them all I'll wear no frown.

Whatever

For your own needs,

Whatever suits,

No matter hearts, no matter soul,

Whatever suits,

To meet your end,

Whatever suits,

No care for others just oneself,

Whatever suits,

Take heed though, we shall all meet at the

Crossroads,

Whatever suits.

Alone

Alone as colours race across the screen,
No matter hearts are bared yet never seen,

As souls are crushed and torn apart,
A promise that will never start,

Fitful sleep and weary days,
The pain that never goes away,

The smile that hides the saddest mind.
The waiting for the end of time,

No light to see in darkest night,
Nothing left an endless flight,

So sit alone and wonder why,
The clouds now fall from empty sky.

I am bought I am sold,

Though I'm fixed I can be turned,

Turn me both you'll not be burned,

In every home I have a place,

But always in the usual space,

I find it strange that you don't see,

Taken for granted that is me.

What am I?

If I could fly I'd like to be,

A simple little bumble bee,

Sipping nectar, making honey,

I have no need for making money,

Creating life I fly around,

Seldom ever on the ground,

I do get tired but seldom sleep,

My zest for life is far too deep.

I stand beneath her leafy canopy,

Mesmerized as thousands of gentle winged

butterflies ignite around me,

Fearlessly they cavort before my eyes,

Resting upon me then off again,

A gentle touch upon my arm,

She is watching me,

Then as quickly as they come they are gone,

The one upon my arm has left her mark on me.

I wrote this poem just for you,

You are so happy never blue,

Pen in hand you work away,

Tireless though the night and day,

So many people you assist,

To get them on the author list,

As you walk now through your barn,

The horses are the ones you charm,

If all the others were like you,

The world would not be in a stew,

So here is a poem just for you,

And thanks for seeing all this through.

If only you knew as I sit here alone.

The thoughts in my head the tears I can't shed.

Of love lost forever of mistakes I can't change,

I reach out to find but touch only air,

I wish but then wake from my dreams,

I look at the liquid and swallow again,

There is no relief though from this type of pain,

We live through our lives with lies and deceit,

The wine will not help me I still shall not sleep,

How many will judge me both now

and when gone,

How many remember the rights not the wrongs,

So let him stand before me

and cast the first stone,

For as darkness surrounds me

then I shall be home.

When all is still when all is calm

When day meets night when night meets day

When life is hard when life is gay

When I see you when you see me

When all is light when all is grey

When I hear when I say

When come the end when comes the start

When time to join when time to part

For soon together all shall be when reached the final

ecstasy.

A wild man of the past, a man not fitting in?

A square peg in a round hole?

A fool, a good man?

Can one be both?

A man of conscience?

A man of care?

A man with no guilt?

A man of extremes?

Who will remember me?

The Phoenix

Mythical creature we stand and stare,
Yet no magic do we see,
The tears the sadness,
For though you hide it well it is there,

Strut as you do confident you are still unsure,
Your plumage bright, irresistible,
Flames surround you the desire to hold your magic,
To taste your flesh and feast upon you,

But yet we fail you, as you fail yourself,
Falling to the ashes in the hope of re-birth.
The flames lick your flesh and pain sears your soul.
The ashes hot and yet you struggle to emerge,

Can a Phoenix fall? Can she just be?
Or will the flames overcome her,
Who knows? She must strive,
Her choices difficult,

Beauty turns to ashes,
Her tears must heal and dowse the flame,
She must choose to arise,
For in the flames she must find her soul,

She must look upon what has been,
Then what is to come.
Cast your eyes no longer on the Phoenix,
Her re-birth must find its own way.

Poppy's Home

Poppy strained her eyes, and looked around, trying to see in the stygian gloom. It had been a long night with little to show for her efforts. If it would just stop raining for a minute she thought. Turning her head towards the sky she searched the unending blackness for the stars, the moon... An airplane, anything, but all she saw were the dark clouds scudding across the heavens obliterating all light. She knew the rain would lash at her regardless. An insignificant speck unnoticed on the giant ball of life. She was so very tired, her legs were weary as she pulled herself up and walked from beneath the shelter of the tree. She almost decided to embrace what little respite was offered by the trees, but the cold that seeped into her body made her mind scream at her to keep going. It was not the night to be out alone. Mud sucked at her feet as she started back down the track that would eventually lead her back to the farm. The wood did offer a little shelter and for that she was grateful. The last mile she knew would be the hardest, there would be no shelter at all, it was all open ground, and there the torrential rain and biting wind could throw their full fury at her. British weather she thought to herself, it was so changeable, it had been a beautiful evening when she had ventured out. Not that she needed to go out.

John and Alice had always provided for her and her family. Poppy valued her independence, even though she wanted for nothing, and was loved as a part of the family as were her three children. As mischievous as they were, they were doted on by John and Alice. She liked to go out at night for her walks, old habits die hard, anyway it kept her slim and she was proud of her figure, it was still lithe and graceful. Childbirth had not ravaged her body as it did some. John and Alice often smiled when her male visitors came to the farm to pay court, even though they knew it was a pointless exercise. John had said often in a seemingly firm voice and the inevitable grin that followed. "I'm sure you encourage them Pops, as pretty as you are I think deep down you're an old tart," and in reply she had given him one of her *WHO ME?* Looks.

Anger began to well up inside her as she thought of her predicament tonight. If it hadn't been for that stupid dog of the Neills, who farmed next door she would be home now. It's appalling she thought. That I should have had to climb a tree, at my age and in this weather to escape a dog because it had such a disagreeable nature. Still she was getting closer to home, sheer determination keeping her going as the cold and wet seemed to seep into her very being. She pushed on, cresting the hill where the tree line ended.

The wind whipped the air from her lungs as she stepped from the relative shelter of the trees, the rain slashing at her eyes, making it almost impossible to see. A mile to go, another ten minutes and she would be home. She was so tired, but knew she had to press on. That bloody dog she thought again, it's all his fault. He should know her by now, she had. after all lived virtually next door for over two years, and what had she ever done to him? Nothing, absolutely nothing, except try to befriend him. It was lucky she could run fast, or she would never have managed to make it to the tree, and God knows what would have happened then. The flush of anger made her adrenalin flow and she increased her efforts to get home, forcing her tired muscles into a trot. Poppy was definitely one of the worlds survivors, she had that certain instinct that took one on when all was lost. Just as it had before she came to live with John and Alice. It had been John and Alice's friends who had found her living rough, half starved, nothing to look forward to except the derision she was given when caught searching for food among the dustbins of the town. How often she had heard the words, "Get out of there, go on you bloody nuisance, go home". Sadness welled up inside her as she thought of the past, she hadn't had a home to go to, how, she had wished she had. She looked up and saw the welcoming light of the farmhouse come into view, and all thoughts save a warm place by the fire and her children vanished. She hurried now, the trot becoming a run. Eager to get to the shelter of the cottage, WOOF, the dogs bark made Poppy jump. A large Collie crossed the yard towards her barking and snarling, then seeing Poppy in the light of the kitchen window rushed over to her, and proceeded to lick her frantically. Jody had fallen in love with Poppy from the moment she had arrived, and Poppy reciprocated those feelings. Jody was a real softy, Poppy had only ever seen her aggressive twice, once when a sales rep had put an arm around Alice in a little too friendly manner. Poppy laughed to herself. He had soon taken his arm away when Jody sank her teeth into his rear. That was certainly one rep that wouldn't be calling again. And once when the Neills dog had strayed into the yard and gone for Poppy, the one and only time he had ever, after the fury of Jodys attack, would ever stray into the yard. She peeled herself away from Jody and entered the door into the kitchen. The door gave its normal, clack, clack, as it swung back into place. Alice's voice came through the warm air, "Poppy is that you?" and the face appeared behind the voice full of concern, "Where have you been, I've been worried sick, out in this weather you silly girl". Poppy made no objection as a big fluffy towel was vigorously applied to dry her.

In fact she responded in her normal manner by rubbing her face against Alice's, her way of saying I love you. Then she curled up in front of the Rayburn with her three kittens vying for the comfiest position. Poppy was home!

Something Completely Different!

Epilogue

I did not want this to be voluminous, simply a short break and the hope that it will provoke thought. it does not matter who you pray to for is it not all the same God whatever man chooses to call him (or her for the feminists). If you take religion as a whole the basis is that one should not only honour this beautiful planet of ours but also the men and women, all creatures that inhabit this globe. I am not a hippy neither am I a vegetarian, I was born an omnivore and shall remain so, just as a lion will always be a carnivore. We all have a purpose, a place, a use. We thought we invented the wheel but in truth it has always been here, we simply developed it for our own convenience, for are we not all wheels within a wheel that turns to keep a balance? The problem is that we do not understand this yet and cannot see that for the wheel to turn for those we leave must be controlled it must be nurtured. Man has only ever been exceptionally good at one thing, an inevitability... death. The really amusing part is we fail to see the inevitability of death for ourselves!

Something Completely Different!
Poems, Proverbs, Rhymes

Chris Dyer
www.chrisdyerauthor.com

About the Author

Although I have always enjoyed writing my love for horses has been instrumental in most of my books, and my knowledge, which I class myself fortunate to have gathered, as it has helped me in my writing. It has also given me the opportunity to formulate natural remedies for horses. I have an association with an international equine products company. Who are very demanding in their requirements, of which I am glad, and I have produced several formulas that I hope they will market once trials are completed. I would say to all that I feel blessed as I am doing the things that I love to do. It is hard work and I have to say it hasn't always been like this... like everyone, there have been serious low points in my life, even to the point of living on a beach wondering where my next meal would come from. I hope as you read this you will have determination and "never say die". Whatever you are doing or wish to do keep at it, there is a strong possibility that if you are determined enough it will come through for you in the end.

www.ingramcontent.com/pod-product-compliance
Lightning Source LLC
Chambersburg PA
CBHW071430040426
42445CB00012BA/1326